Sure Thing

Robin F. Brox

Sure Thing

Robin F. Brox

BlazeVOX [books]
Buffalo, New York

Sure Thing by Robin F. Brox
Copyright © 2011
Published by BlazeVOX [books]

All rights reserved. No part of this book may be reproduced without
the publisher's written permission, except for brief quotations in reviews.
Printed in the United States of America
Book design by Geoffrey Gatza
Cover image by Robin F. Brox

First Edition
ISBN: 978-1-60964-017-0
Library of Congress Control Number: 2011921849

BlazeVOX [books]
76 Inwood Place
Buffalo, NY 14209

Editor@blazevox.org

publisher of weird little books

BlazeVOX [books]

blazevox.org

BlazeVOX

Acknowledgements:

The author would like to thank the following individuals for publishing earlier versions of several poems in this collection: Sam Kaufman, "any paper verse, awry" & "in sixth moment" (*Weather Bell* No. 2, Toronto), John Barlow, "right woven prices," (*Psychic Rotunda*, Toronto), David Hadbawnik, "The Wingspan of Submerged Possibility," "Three Stones," "For All The Other Birds" (*Kadar Koli* 6, Buffalo) & Olive Demetrius for filming "The Wingspan of Submerged Possibility" (used in her documentary *Distaff Descant*, New York). "Call Me a Fitting Name" was first printed as a limited-edition Saucebox chaplet (for the release of Nava Fader's *all the jawing jackdaw*); the title comes from Fader's poem "Will You Eat Gold Eyes for Supper." She would also like to extend heartfelt thanks to Todd Mattina, Naomi Lowinger, Silvana Costa, Kristianne Meal, Becky Moda, Morani Kornberg-Weiss, Aaron Lowinger, Kevin Thurston, Michael Sikkema, Kaplan Harris, David Hadbawnik & Geoffrey Gatza for their inspiration & critical response. Artist photograph by Todd Mattina.

For my parents, Richard & Carole Brox

If they are hungry, feed them
If they write books, read them
—*Kevin Davies*

Sure Thing

from January Jones

Certain heat wave
approaching thirty five
degrees of measure vary
in accuracy of apprehension
western edges about to
melt into bloom, pink-lipp'd
and ice-eyed sun staring
bleak as August's oppression
inverted, swollen throb
of desire haunting
repetition of fingers
where fingers were
longest year fails

To collapse under weight
of time of snowy accumulation
two seas or two keys
frozen solid, solidly into slush
winking shattered moon orb
always recollects, often leaves
or colors changing shades of white
bleached irises or subterranean
cultivations desperately exposed

In thick of forty-some home
games, beard-shrouded lips
circling streets and eerie
lamplight, soft sky cover
making water bodies
right, longitude
varies day-hours,
grease smearing palms, wave
or clasp for safety, orange flash

In bed all night by afternoon
even late morning over
frigid blocks to whiskey
man-crafted, manned now as
then more activity
to mental skeleton, the
moan of crisis
breach of whose silence

What force to be found

early cold forehead

warming to cheek-blush

almost thirty five so

edges verge wider

streets full of icy little rivers, trash clogging

irrepressible downward motion

as lump in throat anticipates loss

tears fleeing eyes undress for chill air

its brick edges funnel, lips prune

And shoulders' wince makes one
miss fervent sic-'em-on attitude
vulgar tenacity, to hope against

darknesses earlier
then later only subtly, myth
for imperceptible change no less
spectacular and radical, perpetuity
of shift, freeze and thaw,
carving out then
carrying away, outdoor
mirror perverts
like crocodile in cornfield
one, official month intent
in its offices

any paper verse, awry

    for Todd Mattina

the straight path to a paradise whips through factories
building dollhouses & miniature cars, not replicas but decoys
filigreed with destruction, false power of an even falser reality

welcome tap of foot-on-path, unbegrudging adoration
for bodies in motion, obvious & persevering in their passions
past rows of production on some smaller scale, onward toward

one place, past forgetting & underneath constructed
surface material, tended as with wishes for good harvest
bound to bounty as in evergreens, the tenacity of burdock

from blind following a need for naught

but revolving, revolution, the pure deep oblivion

of tenderest ambivalences, wet metal aphrodisiac

still rust-proof, unmarred, bare as the dollhouse frame then

layered in gazes & the injury of marked demand or toy chassis

mutating, fluid as fluid, when, to fill low spots like on lawns & sidewalks

submerge to surroundings, outnumbered by digits

repeating, leaves or plumes, cloying lilac or

honeysuckle blown into smokestacks & out as

fantasy, plastic yet remarkably sturdy, worth
study, as is the texture of membranes between worlds,
pink-hued afternoons dawning white-sheeted night

removed not by distance so much as
settlement, homestead of wilderness in ordering
for no stockroom nor wood seller nor way of solicitation

coming again here, & here, misnamed eden
or mastery of fabrication, walkways edged, daisies &
chicory, torrent of waves blooming the guardians of solitude

in sixth moment,

that years could pass by with
speed of months, odd calendar you
may beget of necessity, how like
slowed film quickens action   forwards time,
such potent passivity locks scales even
movement impossibly bound from the first

spring blushes past winter-deep gratifications, first
nights turned last morning, tokens with
smudges and/or near-misspellings more carved even
than written, pulse is urging you
to make   hold   steal   save time
for fabric drowning and the like

accumulate sound or amperaged silence like
lake-effect petals kissing frozen-tongued over first
rocks glasses anxious marching idle time
hurries to a halt brimming with
poverty   euphoria   obscenity   hope that you
finger from calloused palms just even

allowing for residual oils rarer even

though man-made than jitterbug cushion-cut like

talc appetite, stronger current might you

feel inclined to slip   unheeding, first

gust of alfalfa-earth promise sings with

sleeping curl belly stretching leg-length time

contracted, enveloped in overpost cloud-cover time,
something gathers overhead too, and even
under-skin, colored, mechanical, dithering, aged with
laughter or worry perfectly blemished like
circumstance glowing hard and cold, first
flare matching disrupting   line-crossing   changes you

expect the tragic folly returning you
to state-lines, agitating flux of time
late or early   never enough first
moments giving way to waking even
broke beyond attention spoiling trait like
mistaken quarter-song thinks 'to be with'

once each first cleaves living even
beyond bare, you persist extenuating time
accident-tied   thickening like smiles irretrievably   with

Call Me a Fitting Name

no thing
to unfinish   faded
dyed, reddening
a size to forget
seem—less character trait
Honesty for April
tailored, a structured
nothing so apt

no thing (but the idea of)

concrete abstraction

voice sounds room-full

personable, able to

take in   let out

add diamond dart or pleating

off with too-long

for so-long end of

seamstress line, awkward with

thread & needle, sadly

needless, family of

tailor-skill buried

with no things
left in minds
a time to rend and a time
to sow no ideas
but in things pulled close
pinned, like a mute bust
measurements below average

right woven prices

over netting   under fan blades

         over medium   under white cotton

      over table   under rail stop

    over public moment   under April nighttime

over covers   under salad dressing

         over shoulders   under candle wax

      over coffee   under hands

over wireless telephones   under time change

over script   under foot

              over ashtrays filling   under Orion's belt

          over grate shapes   under eyelids

          over series   under black polyester

over burdock wildly   under camera lens

              over tired   under shower heads

over wrists in   under person forest

over ripping out   under stone-skipping

over guest list   under victory garden

over stubble   under weight of

over game scores   under rust spot

over rolling pin   under honey sky

over corner lookout   under massive frames

over masks erupting   under seasonal

over wrought iron cornfield   under nylon

over backless   under bead gravity

over threaded needle   under metal dimensions

over twelve o'clock strike   under whale oil

over glass-bottomed   under hide

over big band under attention span

over silk tie   under scrutiny

                              over smoked meats   under blossom riot

                over quilt pattern   under nails

          over appetizers   under earplug energy

over burn marks   under root tangle

                              over Mohawk Valley   under zoning restriction

          over foreign exchange rates   under sleeplessness over homemade   under Ferris wheels

over low tide   under furrow

   over raw particulars   under tear-stain

  over fast water   under spellbound

 over holiday   under what's wrong

over light deprivation under drenching

  over faces made   under chlorine burn

over dust layer under layers of

over spines ranging under hemline

over border drama-force under piss stained

over sensitive tremble under pipe sweat

over slow dances under gut song

over profiling error under confluence

over bowl passing under feather shackle

over attempted lines   under humidity percentage

over chipped   under ribbon curl

over debate history   under letting go

over garlic peel   under plucked things

over guesses   under absent voice

over rivered desert   under mine cavernings

from January Jones

Days into year, just past
full moon, apple-flesh white
now prone to decay, re-composition
of body strung tighter
taut against cold, effort strain
makes unnatural curvature
but in moments of crisis
you push out where I turn

Concave tension, walks in too-short

sunshine on too-long legs

facing westward pull

into further chill, later setting

children, anchor and buoy

gridlock wilderness has

its own two-step, recipe optional

Year of insistent beginning,
January follows January
while blood clots thick as
thumbs promise what is
is what cannot be

Dreams of hot flowing waters
with, and with oil slick
eddying to echo vacancy
no clear reason but
fear's there, loss only
constant constantly scattering
as seed or feather or secret
growing larger as minutes inch later
you remark on pain of
cure and I simply
cannot tolerate drams
grinning book-jacket and jagged truth
of segregation, sense in
ordering, voyeur to window
winding away, ice thick and darkly

Roar, ream, mirror plays

parts and partings, promise

transparent takes on opaque

layovers, interruptions, table

with kids, bare nut tree or gnawed, rotting pears

of opposing season

now year of opening

reopening, resolutions and novelty

too often overrated or biographies

not yet composed

one of beryl, geology's diary

or books more sincere from

mattresses' positions, how to

wear grooves through snow

banks, to be invisible or just

Still what gets ignored,

raw feet some meatless

storyboard skeleton narrative

black keys echoing not Narcissus

rather chat box chatter multiply

those pleas fall on dear fears

or death nears day inching outward

It wasn't easy, just fate,
attempts aborted, sad purpling
grey scrap of cotton blend
never as wet when alone, lost
soaking, past thunderstorm
fandom or mist and drizzle at
river edge straight in un-
expected direction so expectedly

One echo, one early may I

yes, and blinder against too-bright day in place

overrun with tunneling wind, which

new years' lake resolves to freeze

or promises not to, only one in five

oddity, litany of charred remnant of organic

matter to bars in daytime, cheek-rose cold front,

close fists round initials

Thaw freezes, plummets
to subzero tundra cold
balmy wetness turns bursting pipe
and use value of 'To Resolve'
devolves to guilt at undone
where pride should be piling in drifts
of achievement, to love what
seems barren, to loathe what
narrows and tenses into aching shrug
against cold and toward another

Start, beginnings so arbitrary
that year grows not up like flora
but outward, rippling open
as rings on pond-water
echo of loss to be found eager
for reckless devotions
and western dreams filigreed in
sunset, fingered by arctic air
contact leads to contraction

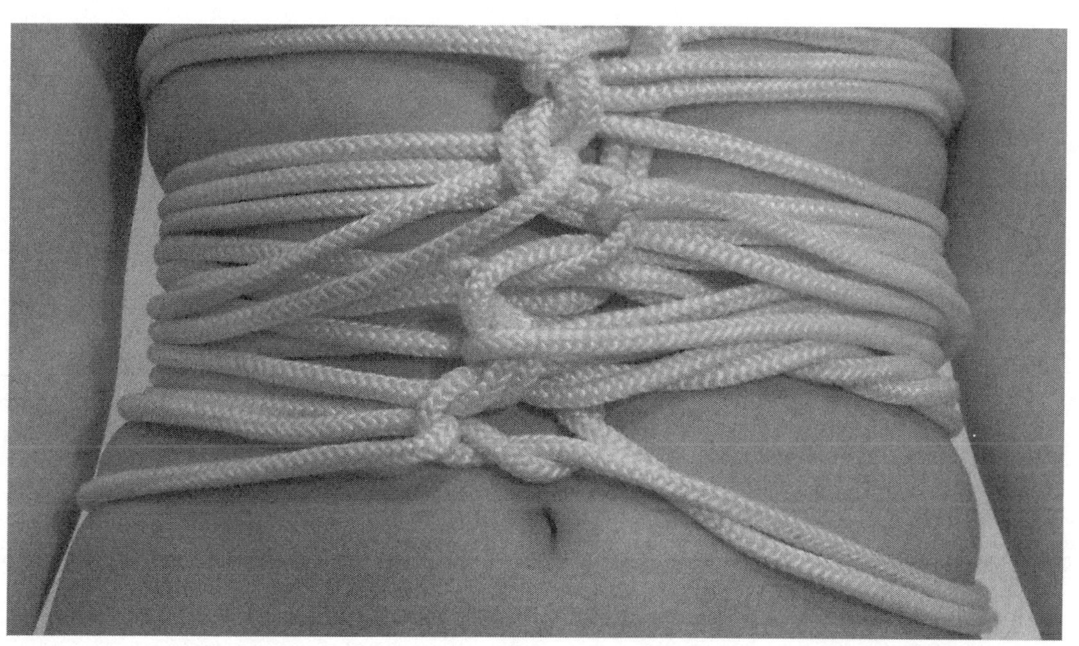

And action slows to staying home
with six-pack, can one institute
driving bans for thoughts
which serve no one well, of failing
to measure up to inane standards
set outside one's self, birds whirl
and chirp on frosty branches, leaves
replaced by feathers, hot little bodies
flashing among shades
of white and gray, cloud mountains
mirrored by shoveled crusts
heaping child-high, hushing
to endure but blanket of
lake effect or nor'easter makes
what could be stay anticipatory

As words wing away, crow's path
not practical but necessary
as epistle burns blue ink over
air, overseas or over time zones
to sway someone or ones, more
often none save internal
companion, cold and ready

Cold forces shoulders forward

motion to which I am no stranger

forward, too forward indeed though

paths turn loops, haunted routes of passage

over, through, back and back again

to blue-porched houses, industrial roofing

or river edge, thinking of spring

ice chunks' dizzy display

makes body feel movement where

none exists, rocking like torsos do

forward, again forward toward

Perfectly nothing days
enough of wildflowers and fowl
give me sharps of ice
impale enduring start
upon its own bravery
undeniable jet stream
pulse pushes ever west to east
what's new, and join in, "I
resolve to sing no songs to-day but
those of manly attachment,"
in hour-piles too fast
as experience's self-made
detritus, constant too-cold for rot save in fruit baskets

Flaring mold in artificial heat

but out one goes no matter

blanked thermometers

to walk is ginger dance-steps over

or meager trudge across

unsure as beginner on skate

blades or forceful bustle in arrogant

defiance of un-shoveled public paths

For higher contrast shortened days
grey and greyer damps feeling, intellect
dulls with tarnish and
may be insulation it nearly compels
hazy distance between living and
alive, important as shade
of meaning between sleep and sleep
with, love and in love, wake awake

To begin against unpreparedness,
hot heart and chill feet
press onward, in shark-doze
or frostbitten sprint

Moving from subtle upwelling

to transit for cataracts, constant

roar of green white-capped

onslaught precipitations wax and wane

as desires do, preferring this

month pomegranates and greens,

no taste for mealy tomato

past sputtering trees in fruitless spin

as if

on impulse   in afternoon wreckage   on alert   in scent memory   on
borrowed plaid   in discomfort   on rambling drop-off   in ink   on purpose
in racing pulse   on wasted eggshells   in secondary sex characteristic   on
DNA sample   in absence   on pillars' tremor   in wordless utterance   on
unlined paper   in danger, sir   on loan   in stone crouch   on tied ice   in fear
of   on strange savvy   in abalone shelter

on margins   in gleaming curl   on stolen real estate   in verging circle   on
moth-wing dust   in repose   on tabletop clutter   in limited view   on
outskirts   in framework trampled   on manual calculation in hollow hoping
on water-bound acreage   in jest   on ambivalent springboard   in nylon sack
on bar stool slumping   in clanging disarray   on shadow slant   in joy pocket
on stiffly leaden   in breath-weight

on frosted meltdown   in guarded confidence   on root   in ruddy sun flare
on one-way streets   in blindered harness lead   on faith less full   in molded
tallow   on sweat stain yellowed   in present tension   on whore's back   in
plastic sheath   on cobblestone ribcage   in closed eye   on display   in mode of
on blue paint   in octagonal artifice   on shouldered well   in searchlight's
blanket   on fog stream

in carelessly   on fist warden   in fumbling buttons   on flaming cheek   in
calculated risk variables   on oil slick   in wooden prism   on matchless
articulation   in peril of   on salted knots   in position   on no upside
in vague griefs   on surging silence   in curve of flesh   on paved nature   in
throbbing thought-hum   on rewind   in laughing motility   on chenille softly
urgent   in absurd review falsehood

on scorpion territory   in root structure   on coastal anomaly   in decency
on magnetized irises   in attic heat   on dream ownership   in upshift   on
heedless impulse   in rush of   on grave platter   in winter thistles   on square
palm   in tongue insisting   on scale truths   in digital remembrance   on
drafting roughly   in greed state   on further reflection   in kite barbarism   on
shifty backtalk   in perpendicular mendacity

on blissful de-capitation   in primate grasp   on conditional return   in flood
money   on rocky river-edge   in secretion aroma   on groundcover   in
porcelain replicas   on forefront   in eager spillage   on edge of fat water
hurtling   in dew deeply   on sugar crust   in page five   on awed lines
in earnest   on wait-weary   in openings able   on projected trestle grass
in dire prediction   on sunset breath passage

in punctuated birds   on some time   in fondness subhuman   on groan wish
in hour snag   on present remove echoing   in absent body   on furred kisses
in chill   on knowledge gravel   in cracks crumbled   on looking   in
unscheduled room   on frantic messages   in maybe crowded   on go-ahead
plank   in beyond torture fantasy   on those old songs   in sadly kept
on posted singular   in chemical orbit   on private matinee

in local strip mine   on forward guard   in volume   on shinier sum   in red
bonus   on unintentional delay   in can't colony   on longitudinal wonder   in
stocking cuff   on improbable finish   in odd equivocal calling   on mercy
thighs   in tighter arms

The Wingspan of Submerged Possibility

for Jennifer Moxley, Silvana Costa & Naomi Lowinger

Here an osprey circles to dive, rising luckless and unsatisfied
An exercise in repetition, in the persistence of a desire
Which demands satisfaction as the glove-slap in a duel
What then is worth such pursuit, shards of heart muscle
Turned to puzzle pieces, what struggle more domestic
Than that at home in the body, a relentless hunger
Two terns fly over the dusk-darkening pond, a pair
Singular and eternal, the dyad of acceptability
Still from the deepening grayscale interval
Between solo and duet, I wring scrapbooks from my mouth

Each tooth, the jaw bone, tongue, lips, gums

Recording their various intimacies, the broken dock thumps

In boats' wake, how honeybees thrust their bodies while feeding,

One appetite, yet what does desire reveal but itself

In each separate act of creation, each chain of chemical reactions

The biology behind love-processes, a set of notebooks for poetry

A diary, thoughts recorded in languages known as other

Drained wine bottles, shots of whiskey, carafes beaded

With the condensation of expectation more often than not

Soured, an unreturned phone call, postcards belatedly

Arriving, pregnant with what is unsaid

Hand on wrist indicates possibility, to lead or follow

Aggressive behavior ensures victory, as being taken,

Overwhelmed, a rooftop or stairwell and kisses

Real or imagined, elevate heart rate, release pheromones

Neurotransmitters in constant attempts at pair bonding

Flawed reason unsupported by the hedonism of the days'

Polyamorous affairs, silly rabbit, monogamy is stupid, these

An unrepentant erotics, but the dishes must get done somehow

Orgasm or not, defiance preferable to the expected

Reproduction, instead the unborn progeny of genius

Ferments, expelled in an ecstasy, a lateral pattern, a chain

Of sensation with loops irregular as the osprey's dive

Its solitary pleasure-seeking complicated by loon calls,

Toward isolation and its end, wisps of smoke and storm-cloud

Wings wide for elevation, each thwarted attempt at satiation

Each success, bittersweet, a thirsty reed

Skin's for tactile learning, overtaking darkness, fatigue

And the hunt ceases, a bird in flight disappearing

Desire's aftertaste an earned hunger, glass-sharp in the shadows

Three Stones

One black
one white one
red smothered
salt water
waves
and faintly scented
insistence, stay
with me
'til memories etch

our names onto each other's skin

we call onyx, obsidian

we call brick, ruby, garnet

my body

in alabaster

what we can and can't

remember or rename.

For All the Other Birds

A labyrinth is
a system of
control (a rope)

a maze
is a method
of confusion   (a blindfold)

lost inside

versus

deliberate

    (meandering

     footstep)

constraint

sweet ease of

intimacy   past

(avalanche of) *wait*

How to get
where I want
to be in
be where
I want to get?

Which is it?
Here or there . . .

from January Jones

Lacking clash of antler for dominance,
here simply submission
giving of self over to winter, cruel
but constant lover (as loss is) strung across
aggregate of days appropriate for
ice hockey and holes cut to fish, no fool's errand
after all, what need we more 'previously frozen'

In weeks stretching out to no end
till another anniversary for firsts

awash in balm to
blistering frigidity and how
many hours of light on incremental
increase, bike lanes closed for piling
snow banks, salt crusting over
refuse, snapped monkey board

Side-view mirrors, bits of paper
plastic wrappers leaching out
until cold snap freezes over, blows
in new mantle of gauze
to dress our annual wound, arctic
air masses swoop in like birds
of prey feasting on Promethean liver
and like that Titan myth our climate
attacks but we regenerate, enduring
too-long nights, bold flashes of sun
glaring in eye-bright sky
how many hours in cars

To equal one, too few in person

nest feathers rustling in

readiness, how need's found one says

from its spinal column, stiff one

not bowed like mine into wind

or blown back in forward lurch

chains on tire contraindicated

by blow, salt and two days ago

river had its precise winter

green skin showing, ethereal surface

more lit from inside, that trickster

light as reflection disguised as

aquamarine underglow, giddy and swollen

light akin to those eyes

glinting under distilled influence

over distance, west and more west

To various edges made by water barrier
landmass escapes scale as month
one endures beyond itself, new beginning
denies end, unending, fed by
scraps of mail, inked notes, ice-rimmed
pools filled with rotting helicopters' dreams

Chill sinks into, up sleeves
down open throats, both filth
of urban winter and freshness
from high pressure system
trees populated with crows
shaking like early autumn leaves
rustle of unrest and thousand eyes
learn this, to face
loathsome February

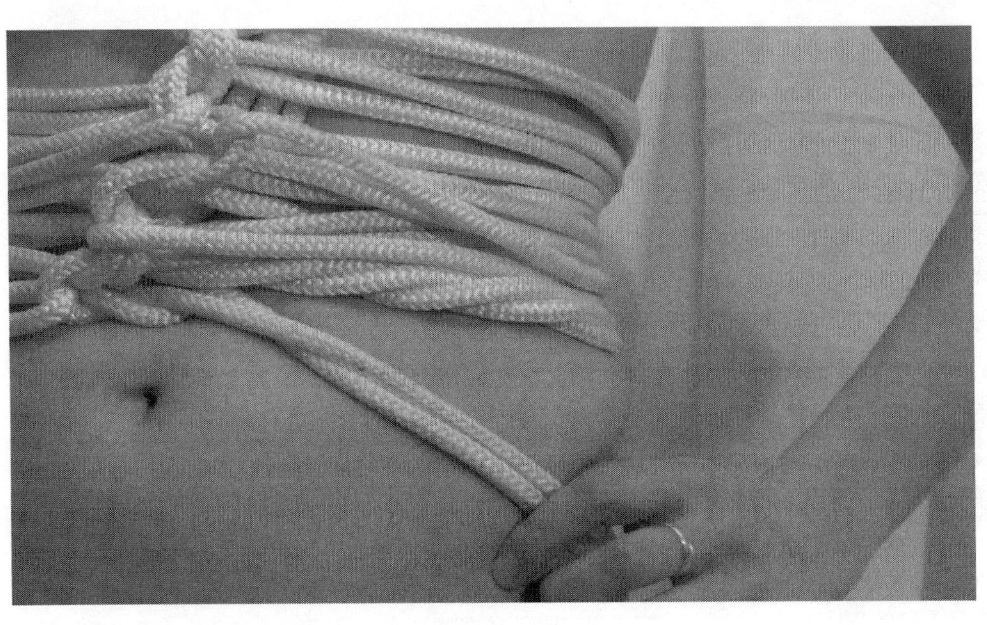

There is no such uncertainty as a sure thing.
—*Robert Burns*

Photography Notes:

p. 32: bricks, 2010

p. 46: rope (1), 2010

p. 57: rope (2), 2010

p. 76: water, 2010

p. 86: Here or There (October 2000 poem, *transcribed by Robert Creeley*), 2011

p. 93: rope (3), 2010

Robin F. Brox was born in 1978. *Sure Thing* is her first full-length book of poems; it contains references to Alice Notley, the NHL, Rainer Maria Rilke, television's *The Simpsons*, the Bay of Fundy, Smokey Robinson & the Miracles, Emily Dickinson, *Coogan's Bluff*, Walt Whitman, & others. A poet & teaching artist, she is the founder of *Saucebox*, a small press & occasional performance series devoted to women artists. She has degrees from SUNY—Buffalo & The University of Maine—Orono. Brox's poems have been or will be published in *Foursquare*, *Stolen Island Review*, *name*, *Artvoice*, *Hemlock*, *Nickel City Nights*, *drill*, *The Buffalo News*, & others; chapbooks include *Who's That Girl* (1999), *Word/Body* (2000, includes color reproduction of paintings by the author), *Saucebox: an anthology of women writers* (2003), *ache* (2003), *Tinsel Strength* (2005), *'s words* (2008), & "When In Doubt, Cowboy Out," a section of the long poem *A. Concoct Key Gush Run*, is available from Binge Press (2011). She may be reached at robinbrox@ymail.com.